The Art of
Negotiation:
Maximizing Profits and Closing Deals

By

John E. Friedland

Copyright© 2023

All rights reserved. Except for the purpose of reviews, radio, and television commentaries. No parts of this publication may be reproduced, stored in a retrieval system, or transmitted in any form or by any means mechanical, photocopying, electronic, recording, etc. Without the permission of the publisher.

Table of Contents

Introduction: Why Negotiation Matters — 3

Chapter 1: The Foundations of Negotiation — 7

Chapter 2: The Psychology of Persuasion — 11

Chapter 3: The Power of Preparation — 15

Chapter 4: Finding Common Ground — 19

Chapter 5: Negotiating for Win-Win Outcomes — 23

Chapter 6: The Art of Listening — 27

Chapter 7: Overcoming Objections — 31

Chapter 8: The Role of Communication in Negotiation — 35

Chapter 9: Tactics and Techniques — 39

Chapter 10: Negotiating Across Cultures 43

Chapter 11: Dealing with Difficult Negotiation Partners 47

Chapter 12: Bringing It All Together 50

Conclusion: Putting the Art of Negotiation into Practice. 53

Introduction: *Why Negotiation Matters*

Negotiation is an essential part of life, both in personal and professional contexts. We negotiate with our family members, friends, and coworkers on a daily basis, whether it's deciding where to go for dinner or discussing a project at work. Negotiation is the process of reaching a mutual agreement between two or more parties, and it is a crucial skill that can impact the outcome of any situation.

In the business world, negotiation is particularly important, as it can make the difference between success and failure. Whether it's negotiating a contract, closing a deal, or resolving a conflict, the ability to negotiate effectively can help individuals and organizations achieve their goals and objectives. Negotiation skills can be used to build stronger relationships, create value, and reach mutually beneficial outcomes.

However, negotiating effectively is not always easy. It requires a deep understanding of human psychology, communication skills, and the ability to navigate complex situations. Negotiation involves managing emotions, building trust, and finding common ground. It also requires the ability to think strategically, plan ahead, and make difficult decisions.

This book is designed to provide a comprehensive guide to the art of negotiation. Through practical examples, expert advice, and proven strategies, readers will learn how to negotiate effectively in a wide range of situations. Whether you are negotiating a business deal, resolving a conflict, or simply trying to improve your personal relationships, the skills, and techniques covered in this book will help you achieve better outcomes and build stronger relationships.

By mastering the art of negotiation, you can become a more effective communicator, problem solver, and decision-maker. Negotiation is a skill that can be learned and improved upon, and the benefits can be profound. So whether you are a seasoned negotiator or just starting out, this book will provide you with the tools and knowledge you need to succeed.

Chapter 1: *The Foundations of Negotiation*

Negotiation is a complex process that involves two or more parties working to reach a mutually beneficial agreement. The foundation of successful negotiation lies in understanding the basics of the negotiation process. In this chapter, we will explore the essential elements of negotiation, including its definition, importance, and types.

The Importance of Negotiation
Negotiation is an essential part of everyday life. We negotiate with our friends, family, and coworkers on a regular basis. Negotiation is particularly important in the business world, where it can impact the success or failure of a company. The ability to negotiate effectively can help organizations build strong relationships, close deals, and resolve conflicts.

Understanding the Basics
The negotiation process involves several key elements. These include

1. Parties: Negotiation involves two or more parties working to reach a mutual agreement.

2. Issues: Negotiation typically involves one or more issues that are being discussed and negotiated.

3. Interests: Each party has interests that they are trying to satisfy through the negotiation process.

4. Alternatives: Each party has alternatives to the negotiated agreement, which they can pursue if the negotiation fails.

5. Standards: Negotiation often involves the use of standards or criteria to guide the negotiation process.

The Different Types of Negotiation

There are several different types of negotiation, each with its own unique characteristics. These include:

1. Distributive Negotiation: In this type of negotiation, the parties are trying to divide a fixed amount of resources. Distributive negotiation is often competitive and can result in a win-lose outcome.

2. Integrative Negotiation: In this type of negotiation, the parties are trying to create value and expand the available resources. Integrative negotiation is often collaborative and can result in a win-win outcome.

3. Multiparty Negotiation: In this type of negotiation, there are more than two parties involved in the negotiation process.

Understanding the foundations of negotiation is essential for success in any negotiation. By recognizing the importance of negotiation, understanding the basics of the process, and identifying the different types of negotiation, individuals and organizations can improve their negotiation skills and achieve better outcomes. In the following chapters, we will delve deeper into the art of negotiation and explore proven strategies and techniques for negotiating effectively in a wide range of situations.

Chapter 2: *The Psychology of Persuasion*

Negotiation is as much about psychology as it is about strategy. In this chapter, we will explore the psychology of persuasion and how it can be used to influence others during a negotiation.

Understanding the Psychology of Persuasion

Persuasion is the art of getting someone to agree with your point of view or take a particular action. Persuasion can be used in negotiation to influence the other party and reach a mutually beneficial agreement. The key principles of persuasion include:

1. Reciprocity: People are more likely to comply with a request if they feel that they owe something in return.

2. Social Proof: People are more likely to comply with a request if they see that others are also complying.

3. Authority: People are more likely to comply with a request if they perceive the person making the request to be an authority figure.

4. Liking: People are more likely to comply with a request if they like the person making the request.

5. Scarcity: People are more likely to comply with a request if they perceive the resource being negotiated as scarce or limited.

Using Persuasion in Negotiation

To use persuasion effectively in negotiation, it is important to understand the other party's perspective and goals. By identifying common ground and using persuasive techniques, negotiators can build trust and influence the other party to reach a mutually beneficial agreement. Some of the most effective persuasion techniques include:

1. Active Listening: By actively listening to the other party, negotiators can gain

valuable insights into their perspectives and build rapport.

2. Framing: Framing involves presenting information in a way that supports your argument and influences the other party's perception of the negotiation.

3. Concession Making: By making small concessions early in the negotiation, negotiators can build trust and create a collaborative environment.

4. Anchoring: Anchoring involves setting a reference point for the negotiation and using it to guide the discussion.

5. Emotion Management: By managing their own emotions and understanding the emotions of the other party, negotiators can create a positive and productive negotiation environment.

The psychology of persuasion is a powerful tool in negotiation. By understanding the principles of persuasion and using effective techniques, negotiators can influence the other party and achieve better outcomes. In the following chapters, we will explore additional strategies and techniques for negotiating effectively in a wide range of situations.

Chapter 3: *The Power of Preparation*

Preparation is the key to successful negotiation. In this chapter, we will explore the importance of preparation and the steps that negotiators can take to prepare effectively.

Why is Preparation Critical?

Preparation is critical to negotiation for several reasons. First, it allows negotiators to develop a clear understanding of their own interests and goals. Second, it enables negotiators to anticipate the other party's interests and goals. Third, it allows negotiators to develop a plan of action and identify potential obstacles to reaching an agreement. Finally, it gives negotiators the confidence to negotiate effectively and achieve a favorable outcome.

Steps for Effective Preparation

To prepare effectively for negotiation, negotiators should take the following steps:

1. Define Your Interests and Goals: Before entering into a negotiation, it is important to have a clear understanding of your own interests and goals. What do you hope to achieve through the negotiation? What are your priorities?

2. Research the Other Party: It is important to research the other party before entering into a negotiation. What are their interests and goals? What is their negotiating style? What are their strengths and weaknesses?

3. Develop a Plan of Action: Based on your interests and goals and your research on the other party, develop a plan of action for the negotiation. Identify your opening position, your concessions, and your ideal outcome.

4. Anticipate Obstacles: Anticipate potential obstacles to reaching an agreement, such as cultural differences, language barriers, or differing priorities. Develop strategies for overcoming these obstacles.

5. Practice: Practice your negotiation skills and techniques before entering into the negotiation. Role-play with a colleague or mentor, or record yourself practicing your negotiation skills.

The Benefits of Preparation

Effective preparation can lead to several benefits in negotiation. First, it can lead to a more productive negotiation, as negotiators are better able to identify common ground and find mutually beneficial solutions. Second, it can lead to a more efficient negotiation, as negotiators are better able to stay focused and avoid unnecessary delays. Finally, it can lead to a more satisfying negotiation, as negotiators are better able to achieve their goals and reach a mutually beneficial agreement.

Preparation is critical to successful negotiation. By defining their interests and goals, researching the other party, developing a plan of action, anticipating obstacles, and practicing their negotiation skills, negotiators can prepare effectively and achieve better outcomes. In the following chapters, we will explore additional strategies and techniques for negotiating effectively in a wide range of situations.

Chapter 4: Finding Common Ground

Negotiation is a process of finding common ground between two parties with different interests and goals. In this chapter, we will explore the importance of finding common ground in negotiation and the strategies and techniques that negotiators can use to achieve this.

Why Finding Common Ground is Important?

Finding common ground is important in negotiation for several reasons. First, it allows negotiators to build trust and rapport with the other party, which can lead to a more productive and efficient negotiation. Second, it can lead to a mutually beneficial agreement that satisfies the interests and goals of both parties. Finally, it can help to reduce conflict and tension in the negotiation, leading to a more positive and satisfying experience for both parties.

Strategies and Techniques for Finding Common Ground

To find common ground in negotiation, negotiators can use a variety of strategies and techniques, including:

1. Active Listening: By actively listening to the other party, negotiators can gain a better understanding of their interests and goals, and identify areas of overlap and agreement.

2. Asking Questions: By asking questions, negotiators can gather more information about the other party's interests and goals, and clarify their own interests and goals.

3. Brainstorming: Brainstorming involves generating a list of potential solutions to the negotiation, without evaluating them. This can help to identify creative solutions that satisfy the interests of both parties.

4. Identifying Shared Values: By identifying shared values between the parties, negotiators can build a foundation of trust and understanding, and find solutions that align with those values.

5. Reframing: Reframing involves looking at the negotiation from a different perspective, and finding common ground based on that perspective.

The Benefits of Finding Common Ground

Finding common ground in negotiation can lead to several benefits. First, it can lead to a more productive and efficient negotiation, as negotiators are better able to identify mutually beneficial solutions. Second, it can lead to a more satisfying negotiation experience, as both parties feel that their interests and goals have been met. Finally, it can lead to a stronger and more positive relationship between the parties, which can be beneficial in future negotiations.

Conclusion

Finding common ground is a critical component of successful negotiation. By using strategies and techniques such as active listening, asking questions, brainstorming, identifying shared values, and reframing, negotiators can build trust and rapport, identify mutually beneficial solutions, and achieve a more satisfying negotiation outcome. In the following chapters, we will explore additional strategies and techniques for negotiating effectively in a wide range of situations.

Chapter 5: *Negotiating for Win-Win Outcomes*

Negotiating for win-win outcomes is a strategy that focuses on creating mutually beneficial solutions for all parties involved in the negotiation. In this chapter, we will explore the importance of win-win negotiation, the key principles of this approach, and the techniques that negotiators can use to achieve this outcome.

Why Win-Win Negotiation Matters?

Win-win negotiation is important because it helps to build positive relationships between the parties, fosters cooperation, and collaboration, and creates a more sustainable and long-lasting agreement. It also allows both parties to feel that their interests and goals have been met, leading to a more satisfying negotiation experience.

Key Principles of Win-Win Negotiation

The key principles of win-win negotiation include:

1. Focus on Interests, Not Positions: Negotiators should focus on the underlying interests and needs of both parties, rather than on their stated positions.

2. Create Value: Negotiators should strive to create value by identifying opportunities for mutual gain and exploring creative solutions.

3. Build Relationships: Negotiators should focus on building trust and rapport between the parties, which can lead to more productive and efficient negotiations.

4. Share Information: Negotiators should be transparent and share information openly, which can help to build trust and lead to more informed decision-making.

Techniques for Achieving Win-Win Outcomes

To achieve win-win outcomes in negotiation, negotiators can use a variety of techniques, including:

1. Expanding the Pie: By looking for opportunities to create value for both parties, negotiators can expand the potential outcomes of the negotiation.

2. Tradeoffs: Negotiators can identify areas where each party is willing to make concessions in order to achieve a mutually beneficial agreement.

3. Package Deals: Negotiators can bundle several issues together to create a package deal that meets the interests of both parties.

4. Collaborative Problem-Solving: Negotiators can work together to solve problems and find creative solutions that meet the interests of both parties.

The Benefits of Win-Win Negotiation

Win-win negotiation can lead to several benefits, including a more productive and efficient negotiation, a more satisfying negotiation experience, and a stronger and more positive relationship between the parties. It can also lead to a more sustainable and long-lasting agreement, as both parties feel that their interests and goals have been met.

Conclusion

Negotiating for win-win outcomes is a powerful strategy that can lead to more positive and productive negotiations. By focusing on the key principles of win-win negotiation and using techniques such as expanding the pie, tradeoffs, package deals, and collaborative problem-solving, negotiators can create solutions that meet the interests of both parties. In the following chapters, we will explore additional strategies and techniques for negotiating effectively in a wide range of situations.

Chapter 6: *The Art of Listening*

Listening is a critical skill in negotiation, yet it is often overlooked or undervalued. In this chapter, we will explore the importance of active listening in negotiation, the key elements of effective listening, and techniques that negotiators can use to become better listeners.

Why Listening Matters?

Active listening is a crucial aspect of effective negotiation. It allows negotiators to understand the interests, needs, and concerns of the other party, which is essential for finding common ground and creating mutually beneficial outcomes. By listening actively, negotiators can also build trust and rapport, which can lead to more productive and efficient negotiations.

Key Elements of Effective Listening

Effective listening involves several key elements, including:

1. Focus: Good listeners pay attention to the speaker, avoiding distractions and interruptions.

2. Empathy: Effective listeners seek to understand the perspective and feelings of the speaker.

3. Clarification: Good listeners seek to clarify the speaker's message, asking questions to ensure understanding.

4. Feedback: Effective listeners provide feedback to the speaker, indicating that they have understood their message.

Techniques for Becoming a Better Listener

To become a better listener, negotiators can use several techniques, including:

1. Paraphrasing: Restating the speaker's message in one's own words to confirm understanding.

2. Reflective Listening: Reflecting back on the feelings or emotions expressed by the speaker.

3. Asking Open-Ended Questions: Encouraging the speaker to share more information.

4. Avoiding Assumptions: Not assuming what the speaker means, but asking for clarification.

The Benefits of Effective Listening

Effective listening can lead to several benefits in negotiation, including a better understanding of the other party's interests and needs, building trust and rapport, and identifying opportunities for mutual gain. It also leads to better problem-solving and decision-making, as all parties feel heard and valued.

Conclusion

Active listening is a critical skill in negotiation, and effective negotiators must master this skill to achieve successful outcomes. By focusing on the key elements of effective listening and using techniques such as paraphrasing, reflective listening, and asking open-ended questions, negotiators can become better listeners and improve their negotiation skills. In the following chapters, we will explore additional strategies and techniques for negotiating effectively in a wide range of situations.

Chapter 7: *Overcoming Objections*

In negotiation, objections are a common occurrence. They can come in many forms, including skepticism, resistance, and pushback. These objections can be challenging to navigate, but skilled negotiators know how to overcome them and move toward a successful outcome. In this chapter, we will discuss strategies for overcoming objections in negotiation.

Understanding Objections

Before we can overcome objections, we must first understand what they are and why they arise. Objections are concerns or issues raised by the other party that need to be addressed before they can agree to a proposed solution. They can be related to the offer itself, the negotiation process, or personal factors such as values and preferences.

Strategies for Overcoming Objections

Effective negotiators have several strategies for overcoming objections, including:

1. Acknowledge the objection: The first step in overcoming an objection is to acknowledge it. This shows the other party that their concern is being heard and taken seriously.

2. Clarify the objection: Once an objection is acknowledged, it's essential to clarify precisely what the other party's concern is. This ensures that you understand the issue and can address it effectively.

3. Address the objection: Once the objection is clear, it's time to address it. This may involve providing additional information, modifying the proposal, or finding alternative solutions.

4. Use persuasive techniques: Skilled negotiators also use persuasive techniques to overcome objections. This may involve appealing to the other party's values or interests, using social proof, or finding common ground.

Tips for Overcoming Objections

Negotiators can also use several tips to overcome objections effectively, including:

1. Anticipate objections: Experienced negotiators often anticipate objections and plan ahead to address them.

2. Keep emotions in check: It's important to stay calm and composed when addressing objections to avoid escalating the situation.

3. Be flexible: Negotiators should be open to modifying their proposals or finding alternative solutions to address objections.

4. Avoid ultimatums: Ultimatums can be counterproductive in negotiation, so it's best to avoid them.

Conclusion

Objections are a natural part of the negotiation, and effective negotiators know how to overcome them. By understanding objections, using effective strategies such as acknowledging, clarifying, and addressing the concern, and using persuasive techniques, negotiators can overcome objections and move toward a successful outcome. In the next chapter, we will discuss negotiation tactics and strategies that can be used to achieve favorable outcomes.

Chapter 8: *The Role of Communication in Negotiation*

Communication is a vital component of successful negotiation. Skilled negotiators know how to use communication effectively to build rapport, share information, and persuade the other party. In this chapter, we will discuss the role of communication in negotiation and strategies for improving communication skills.

The Importance of Communication in Negotiation

Effective communication is crucial in the negotiation because it helps to:

1. Build rapport: Building rapport is essential for creating a positive negotiation environment and establishing trust between parties.

2. Share information: Negotiation involves exchanging information, and effective communication is necessary to ensure

that information is accurately and clearly conveyed.

3. Persuade the other party: Persuasion is a key aspect of negotiation, and effective communication is necessary to convince the other party of the benefits of a proposed solution.

4. Resolve conflicts: Communication skills are essential for resolving conflicts that may arise during negotiation.

Improving Communication Skills in Negotiation

To improve communication skills in negotiation, negotiators can use several strategies, including:

1. Active listening: Active listening involves paying attention to what the other party is saying, asking questions, and clarifying information to ensure mutual understanding.

2. Effective questioning: Asking open-ended questions can help elicit more detailed information and encourage the other party to share their perspective.

3. Nonverbal communication: Nonverbal cues such as body language, tone of voice, and facial expressions can convey information and emotions that are not explicitly stated.

4. Use of language: Effective communication in negotiation involves using clear, concise language and avoiding jargon or technical terms that may confuse the other party.

5. Empathy: Empathy involves understanding and considering the other party's perspective and feelings, which can help build rapport and create a positive negotiation environment.

Conclusion

Effective communication is essential for successful negotiation. By understanding the importance of communication in negotiation and using strategies such as active listening, effective questioning, nonverbal communication, and empathy, negotiators can improve their communication skills and achieve better negotiation outcomes. In the next chapter, we will discuss the importance of ethics and trust in negotiation.

Chapter 9: *Tactics and Techniques*

Negotiation tactics and techniques are the strategies and methods used to influence the other party in a negotiation. While some tactics can be unethical and manipulative, others can help negotiators achieve their desired outcomes while maintaining a positive negotiation environment. In this chapter, we will discuss different negotiation tactics and techniques and their effectiveness in achieving negotiation objectives.

1. Competitive tactics: Competitive tactics involve using aggressive or confrontational strategies to gain an advantage in negotiation. Examples include making extreme demands, threatening to walk away from the negotiation, and using ultimatums. While these tactics can be effective in certain situations, they can also damage relationships and lead to negative outcomes.

2. Cooperative tactics: Cooperative tactics involve using a collaborative and problem-solving approach to negotiation. Examples include brainstorming solutions, offering concessions, and finding areas of common ground. These tactics can be effective in building rapport and trust between parties and can lead to win-win outcomes.

3. Persuasive tactics: Persuasive tactics involve using language and arguments to influence the other party. Examples include using logic and reason to support a proposal, appealing to the other party's emotions, and using social proof to show the benefits of a proposed solution. These tactics can be effective in convincing the other party to agree to a proposal.

4. Integrative tactics: Integrative tactics involve finding creative solutions that meet the needs and interests of both parties. Examples include expanding the negotiation agenda to include additional issues, exploring multiple options, and

identifying trade-offs that benefit both parties. These tactics can lead to win-win outcomes and can help build long-term relationships between parties.

5. Ethical tactics: Ethical tactics involve using honest and transparent strategies in negotiation. Examples include disclosing relevant information, avoiding deception or manipulation, and respecting the other party's interests and needs. These tactics can help build trust and credibility between parties and can lead to positive negotiation outcomes.

Conclusion

Negotiation tactics and techniques are essential skills for successful negotiation. By understanding the different types of tactics and techniques available and their effectiveness in achieving negotiation objectives, negotiators can choose the best approach for their specific situation. While some tactics can be unethical and damaging to relationships, cooperative, persuasive, integrative, and ethical tactics can lead to positive negotiation outcomes and long-term relationships. In the next chapter, we will discuss the importance of managing emotions in negotiation.

Chapter 10: *Negotiating Across Cultures*

Negotiating across cultures can be challenging as different cultures have unique values, beliefs, and communication styles. A lack of understanding of cultural differences can lead to misunderstandings, breakdowns in communication, and failed negotiations. In this chapter, we will discuss how to negotiate successfully across cultures.

1. Understanding cultural differences: To negotiate successfully across cultures, it is essential to understand the cultural differences that exist. Different cultures may have different communication styles, negotiation goals, and expectations. For example, in some cultures, building a personal relationship before entering into business negotiations is essential, while in others, negotiations are strictly business.

2. Building rapport: Building rapport is an essential component of negotiation

across cultures. Building trust and establishing a relationship with the other party can help break down barriers and improve communication. This can involve learning about the other culture, showing respect and appreciation for their culture, and finding common ground.

3. Adapting communication styles: Communication styles differ across cultures, and it is important to adapt communication styles to fit the other party's culture. For example, in some cultures, indirect communication is preferred, while in others, direct communication is necessary. It is essential to understand the cultural norms around communication and adapt accordingly.

4. Handling differences: Differences may arise during cross-cultural negotiations, and it is important to handle them effectively. This involves understanding the other party's perspective, finding areas of common ground, and being

willing to compromise. It is also essential to avoid cultural misunderstandings that may lead to offense.

5. Building cultural competence: Building cultural competence involves developing an understanding of different cultures and their negotiation styles. This may involve learning about different cultures, building relationships with people from different cultures, and being willing to adapt negotiation styles to fit different cultural contexts.

Conclusion

Negotiating across cultures requires an understanding of cultural differences, building rapport, adapting communication styles, handling differences effectively, and building cultural competence. By developing cultural competence and adapting negotiation styles to fit different cultural contexts, negotiators can overcome cultural barriers and achieve successful negotiation outcomes. In the next chapter, we will discuss the importance of ethical behavior in negotiation.

Chapter 11: *Dealing with Difficult Negotiation Partners*

Negotiations can be challenging when dealing with difficult negotiation partners. These are individuals who are aggressive, uncooperative, or difficult to work with. In this chapter, we will discuss strategies for dealing with difficult negotiation partners.

1. Stay Calm: It is essential to remain calm and composed when dealing with difficult negotiation partners. It is easy to become frustrated or angry when dealing with someone who is uncooperative, but this can lead to a breakdown in communication and a failed negotiation.

2. Listen Actively: Active listening is crucial when dealing with difficult negotiation partners. It involves paying attention to what the other party is saying, clarifying any misunderstandings, and trying to understand their perspective.

3. Focus on Interests: It is important to focus on the interests of both parties rather than positions when dealing with difficult negotiation partners. By identifying shared interests, it is possible to find common ground and negotiate a mutually beneficial agreement.

4. Stay Professional: It is essential to maintain a professional demeanor when dealing with difficult negotiation partners. This involves avoiding personal attacks or insults and focusing on the negotiation objectives.

5. Use Tactics and Techniques: Negotiators can use various tactics and techniques when dealing with difficult negotiation partners, such as taking breaks, exploring alternatives, or bringing in a neutral third party.

6. Consider Walking Away: In some cases, it may be necessary to consider walking away from a negotiation if dealing with a difficult negotiation partner. This may be the best option if the other party is not

willing to negotiate in good faith or if an agreement cannot be reached.

Conclusion

Dealing with difficult negotiation partners can be challenging, but by staying calm, actively listening, focusing on interests, maintaining professionalism, using tactics and techniques, and considering walking away when necessary, it is possible to negotiate successfully even in challenging situations. In the next chapter, we will discuss the importance of trust in negotiation.

Chapter 12: *Bringing It All Together*

Negotiation is a complex process that involves a range of skills, tactics, and strategies. In this chapter, we will bring together the key concepts discussed in this book to help you negotiate effectively and achieve your objectives.

1. Understand the Process: It is essential to have a clear understanding of the negotiation process, including the key stages, participants, and objectives. By understanding the process, you can develop a strategy that will help you achieve your goals.

2. Develop Your Skills: Negotiation is a skill that can be developed and improved over time. By practicing active listening, questioning, and persuasion techniques, you can become a more effective negotiator.

3. Focus on Interests: Focusing on interests rather than positions is a key strategy for

successful negotiation. By identifying shared interests, you can find common ground and negotiate a mutually beneficial agreement.

4. Prepare Thoroughly: Preparation is critical to successful negotiation. This involves researching the other party, identifying your objectives, and developing a clear strategy and plan for the negotiation.

5. Communicate Effectively: Effective communication is crucial in negotiation. By using clear and concise language, active listening, and asking open-ended questions, you can ensure that you understand the other party's perspective and can convey your own effectively.

6. Be Creative: Sometimes, traditional negotiation tactics may not work. In these situations, it is essential to be creative and think outside the box. Brainstorming and exploring alternatives can help you find new solutions to challenging problems.

7. Build Trust: Trust is a critical component of successful negotiation. By demonstrating integrity, being transparent, and following through on your commitments, you can build trust with the other party and increase the likelihood of a successful negotiation.

Conclusion

Negotiation is a challenging but rewarding process that requires a range of skills and strategies. By understanding the negotiation process, developing your skills, focusing on interests, preparing thoroughly, communicating effectively, being creative, and building trust, you can negotiate successfully and achieve your objectives. With practice and experience, you can become a skilled negotiator and achieve great results in your personal and professional life.

Conclusion: Putting the Art of Negotiation into Practice.

Negotiation is an essential skill for success in both personal and professional settings. By mastering the art of negotiation, you can achieve your objectives, build strong relationships, and overcome challenges.

Throughout this book, we have explored the foundations of negotiation, the psychology of persuasion, the power of preparation, finding common ground, negotiating for win-win outcomes, the art of listening, overcoming objections, the role of communication, tactics, and techniques, negotiating across cultures, and dealing with difficult negotiation partners. We have provided practical tips and strategies to help you negotiate effectively and achieve your goals.

Now that you have learned about the art of negotiation, it is time to put it into practice. Start by setting clear objectives for your negotiation, identifying the other party's interests, and developing a clear strategy and plan. Prepare thoroughly, including researching the other party, anticipating objections, and developing alternative solutions.

During the negotiation, focus on interests rather than positions, listen actively, and communicate effectively. Be creative and flexible, and look for opportunities to build trust and find mutually beneficial solutions.

Remember that negotiation is not about winning or losing, but about finding a solution that works for both parties. By approaching negotiation with a collaborative and problem-solving mindset, you can build strong relationships and achieve great results.

So go forth and practice the art of negotiation. With time and experience, you will become a skilled negotiator and achieve success in all aspects of your life.